MW00366466

To:_____

From: _____

Other Books by Gregory E. Lang

Why A Daughter Needs A Dad

GREGORY E. LANG

WITH PHOTOGRAPHS BY JANET LANKFORD-MORAN

CUMBERLAND HOUSE™

To Meagan, the inspiration for what
I do right, the reason I try
to do no wrong.—Dad

For my dad, who fostered creativity,
and Helen, who gave guidance at
just the right time.—Janet

Copyright © 2002, 2011 by Gregory E. Lang and Janet Lankford-Moran
Cover and internal design © 2011 by Sourcebooks, Inc.
Photographs by Janet Lankford-Moran
Sourcebooks and the colophon are registered trademarks of
Sourcebooks, Inc.

Published by Cumberland House, an imprint of Sourcebooks, Inc.
P.O. Box 4410, Naperville, Illinois 60567-4410
(630) 961-3900
Fax: (630) 961-2168
www.sourcebooks.com

Printed and bound in China.
OGP 10 9 8 7 6

Why A Daughter Needs A Dad

A daughter needs a dad

to learn that when he says it
will be okay soon, it will.

A daughter
needs a dad...

who will always have time to
give her hugs and kisses.

who does not mind when she
steps on his shoes while dancing.

A daughter needs a dad

to teach her that her value
as a person is more than
the way she looks.

A daughter
needs a dad...

to protect her from scary
nighttime creatures.

to answer the questions that
keep her awake at night.

to protect her from
thunder and lightning.

A daughter needs a dad

so she will know what it is like
to be somebody's favorite.

A daughter

needs a dad...

to join her journey when she
is too afraid to walk alone.

to teach her the meaning
of integrity, and how to
avoid the crooked path.

A daughter needs a dad

to teach her that family is
more important than work.

A daughter needs a dad

to be the standard against
which she will judge all men.

A daughter

needs a dad...

to teach her the difference
between being firm
and being stubborn.

to teach her that respect is to
be earned, as he has earned hers.

to teach her that she is
equal to her husband.

A daughter needs a dad

to tuck her in at night.

A daughter
needs a dad...

to help her take the risks that
will build her confidence.

to help her try again
whenever she fails.

A daughter needs a dad

to be the history of her
family for her own children.

A daughter

needs a dad...

to give her the guidance
she needs as she begins to
resolve her own troubles.

to pull her back when she is
headed in the wrong direction.

A daughter needs a dad

to remind her of what she
may not remember.

A daughter
needs a dad...

to teach her to recognize
truth and reward it.

to teach her to recognize
sincerity and encourage it.

A daughter needs a dad

to give her the gentle pushes
that help her grow.

A daughter needs a dad

who teaches her she is
important by stopping what
he is doing to watch her.

A daughter
needs a dad...

to teach her how things work.

to show her how to fix
things for herself.

A daughter needs a dad

to teach her the importance
of being a lady.

to teach her to stand up
for herself.

A daughter
needs a dad...

to help around the house so
that her mother will have time
to spend with her, too.

to teach her that her role
in a family is greater than
the work she does.

A daughter needs a dad

to teach her the joy
of serving others.

A daughter
needs a dad...

to teach her not to let
pride get in the way of
discovering new things.

to teach her to experiment
for the sake of testing
her own assumptions.

A daughter needs a dad

to show her that true
love is unconditional.

A daughter
needs a dad...

to tell her all she needs
to know about boys.

to show her that all boys are
not like the one who hurt her.

to teach her how to
recognize a gentleman.

A daughter needs a dad

to teach her that men and women can be good friends.

to teach her about fairness.

A daughter
needs a dad...

to teach her what kind of
man to choose to be the
father of her children.

to stand with her on the day
she marries the man she hopes
will be just like her father.

A daughter needs a dad

to teach her that loving
her family is a priority.

A daughter
needs a dad...

to teach her to learn
from her experiences.

to help her find her way.

to share with her the wisdom
she has not yet acquired.

A daughter needs a dad

to teach her when
to be cautious.

to make the tough decisions
for her until she is able to
make them for herself.

A daughter

needs a dad...

to show her the benefits
of hard work.

to teach her to spend responsibly,
save for a rainy day, and give
with a generous heart.

A daughter needs a dad

so she learns that men
can be trustworthy.

A daughter
needs a dad...

to give her a strong,
willful character.

to teach her how to focus her
mind in the midst of distraction.

A daughter needs a dad

to carry her just because
she wants to be carried.

A daughter needs a dad

to teach her what it means
to always be there.

A daughter

needs a dad...

to teach her that a man's
strength is not the force
of his hand or his voice, but
the kindness of his heart.

to set a moral standard for her.

A daughter needs a dad

to tell her truthfully that she
is the most beautiful of all.

A daughter needs a dad

■　　　■　　　■　　　■　　　■　　　■　　　■

because without him she will have
less in her life than she deserves.

To Contact the Author

Write in care of the publisher:
Gregory E. Lang
c/o Sourcebooks, Inc.
P.O. Box 4410
Naperville, IL 60567-4410

Email the author or visit his website:
gregoryelang@gmail.com
www.gregoryelang.com

Email the photographer or visit her website:
janet@oijoyphoto.com
www.oijoyphoto.com